CONTENTS

SALMON BITES

PREP: 10 min. \ **TOTAL:** 10 min. \ **MAKES:** 7 servings

---

7 slices dense pumpernickel bread

½ cup (½ of 8-oz. tub) *Philadelphia* Cream Cheese Spread

2 Tbsp. chopped fresh dill

3.5 oz. smoked salmon

1 Use 1¾-inch cookie cutter to cut 4 rounds out of each bread slice. Discard bread trimmings or reserve for another use.

2 Mix cream cheese spread with dill; spread over bread. Top with salmon.

SPECIAL EXTRA

Garnish each topped bread round with a sprig of fresh dill.

ZESTY STUFFED OLIVES

PREP: 10 min. \ **TOTAL:** 10 min. \ **MAKES:** 10 servings

½ **cup (½ of 8-oz. tub)** *Philadelphia* **Cream Cheese Spread**

20 **colossal black olives**

2 **Tbsp.** *Kraft* **Zesty Italian Dressing**

2 **Tbsp. chopped fresh parsley**

1 **Spoon** cream cheese spread into small resealable plastic bag. Press cream cheese into one of the bottom corners of bag. Cut off small piece from corner of bag. Squeeze cream cheese into centers of olives.

2 **Place** olives on serving plate. Drizzle with dressing. Sprinkle with parsley.

SPRING VEGGIE PIZZA APPETIZER

PREP: 15 min. \ **TOTAL:** 2 hours 58 min. \ **MAKES:** 32 servings

---

2 pkg. (8 oz. each) refrigerated crescent dinner rolls

1 tub (8 oz.) *Philadelphia* ⅓ Less Fat than Cream Cheese

½ cup *Miracle Whip* Dressing

1 tsp. dill weed

½ tsp. onion powder

1 cup each chopped sugar snap peas and quartered cherry tomatoes

½ cup each sliced radishes, chopped yellow peppers and shredded carrots

3 green onions, chopped

1 **Heat** oven to 375°F.

2 **Unroll** each package of dough into 2 rectangles. Press onto bottom and up sides of 15×10×1-inch pan to form crust, firmly pressing seams and perforations together to seal.

3 **Bake** 11 to 13 min. or until golden brown; cool.

4 **Mix** reduced-fat cream cheese, dressing and seasonings until blended; spread onto crust. Top with remaining ingredients. Refrigerate 2 hours.

FESTIVE FAVORITE LAYERED DIP

PREP: 10 min. \ **TOTAL:** 10 min. \ **MAKES:** 6 cups or 48 servings, 2 Tbsp. each

---

- **1 tub (8 oz.)** *Philadelphia* **Cream Cheese Spread**
- **½ cup** *Breakstone's* **or** *Knudsen* **Sour Cream**
- **¼ cup** *Miracle Whip* **Dressing**
- **1 cup** *Taco Bell* **Home Originals** **Thick 'N Chunky Salsa**
- **1 pkg. (8 oz.)** *Kraft* **Shredded Mozzarella Cheese**
- **1 green pepper, finely chopped**
- **2 tomatoes, chopped**
- **2 green onions, chopped**

1 **Mix** first 3 ingredients until blended; spread onto bottom of shallow bowl.

2 **Top** with layers of all remaining ingredients.

Taco Bell and *Home Originals* are trademarks owned and licensed by Taco Bell Corp.

MAKE AHEAD
Dip can be stored in refrigerator up to 2 hours before serving.

SERVING SUGGESTION
Serve with crackers.

BAKED CRAB RANGOON

PREP: 20 min. \ **TOTAL:** 40 min. \ **MAKES:** 12 servings

- **1** can (6 oz.) crabmeat, drained, flaked
- **4** oz. (½ of 8-oz. pkg.) *Philadelphia* Neufchâtel Cheese, softened
- **¼** cup *Kraft* Light Mayo Reduced Fat Mayonnaise
- **2** green onions, thinly sliced
- **12** won ton wrappers

1 **Heat** oven to 350°F.

2 **Mix** first 4 ingredients until blended.

3 **Line** each of 12 muffin cups sprayed with cooking spray with 1 won ton wrapper, allowing edge of wrapper to extend over top. Fill with crab mixture.

4 **Bake** 18 to 20 min. or until edges are golden brown and filling is heated through.

FOR CRISPIER RANGOONS

Bake won ton wrappers in muffin cups at 350°F for 5 to 7 min. or until lightly browned. Fill with crabmeat mixture and bake 6 to 8 min. or until filling is heated through.

CHICKEN & CRANBERRY BITES

PREP: 10 min. \ **TOTAL:** 25 min. \ **MAKES:** 24 servings

---

  1 pkg. (17.3 oz.) frozen puff pastry (2 sheets), thawed

  ¾ cup (¾ of 8-oz. tub) *Philadelphia* Cream Cheese Spread

1½ cups chopped cooked chicken breasts

  ½ cup canned whole berry cranberry sauce

1 **Heat** oven to 425°F.

2 **Roll** out 1 pastry sheet on lightly floured surface into 12-inch square; cut into 12 smaller squares. Place in single layer on lightly floured baking sheet. Repeat with remaining pastry sheet.

3 **Spoon** 1½ tsp. cream cheese spread onto center of each pastry square. Top with chicken and cranberry sauce.

4 **Bake** 14 to 15 min. or until pasty is golden brown, rotating baking sheet after 7 min.

HOW TO CUT PUFF PASTRY
Use a pizza cutter to easily cut the pastry dough into squares.

PESTO CROSTINI

PREP: 20 min. \ **TOTAL:** 20 min. \ **MAKES:** 16 servings

- ⅓ cup *Kraft* Italian Vinaigrette Dressing
- 3 cups fresh basil leaves
- ⅓ cup *Kraft* Grated Parmesan Cheese
- 32 baguette slices (¼ inch thick), toasted
- 1 tub (8 oz.) *Philadelphia* Cream Cheese Spread
- ¼ cup *Kraft* Grated Parmesan Cheese

1 Blend dressing, basil and ⅓ cup Parmesan in blender until smooth.

2 Spread toast slices with cream cheese spread, then basil mixture.

3 Sprinkle with ¼ cup Parmesan.

STORAGE KNOW-HOW

Wrap stems of basil in damp paper towel; place in resealable plastic bag and refrigerate up to 4 days. Or place the bunch, stem-ends down, in a glass of water; cover with a plastic bag and refrigerate as directed.

CREAMY MEDITERRANEAN SPREAD

PREP: 10 min. \ **TOTAL:** 10 min. \ **MAKES:** 3 cups or 24 servings, 2 Tbsp. each

---

1 pkg. (8 oz.) *Philadelphia* Cream Cheese, softened

1 jar (7 oz.) roasted red peppers, drained, chopped

1 pkg. (4 oz.) *Athenos* Traditional Crumbled Feta Cheese

½ cup chopped kalamata olives (about 40)

¼ cup *Kraft* Balsamic Vinaigrette Dressing

2 Tbsp. chopped fresh parsley

1 Spread cream cheese onto bottom of shallow dish.

2 Combine remaining ingredients; spoon over cream cheese.

SERVING SUGGESTION
Serve with crackers.

RUSTIC CARMELIZED ONION TART

PREP: 10 min. \ **TOTAL:** 1 hour \ **MAKES:** 10 servings

4 slices *Oscar Mayer* **Bacon, cut into 1-inch pieces**

1 **large onion, thinly sliced**

1 **ready-to-use refrigerated pie crust (½ of 14.1-oz. pkg.)**

1 **pkg. (8 oz.)** *Philadelphia* **Cream Cheese, softened**

¼ cup *Breakstone's* or *Knudsen* **Sour Cream**

½ cup *Kraft* **2% Milk Shredded Swiss Cheese**

1 **Cook** bacon in large skillet on medium-high heat 5 min. or just until bacon is crisp, stirring occasionally. Remove bacon from skillet with slotted spoon, reserving drippings in skillet. Drain bacon on paper towels; set aside. Add onions to drippings; cook 15 to 20 min. or until onions are caramelized, stirring frequently.

2 **Heat** oven to 400°F. Unroll pie crust on baking sheet. Mix cream cheese and sour cream; spread onto crust. Spoon onion mixture and bacon onto center of crust, leaving 2-inch border; top with Swiss cheese. Fold border over filling, leaving opening in center and pleating crust as necessary to fit.

3 **Bake** 20 to 25 min. or until crust is lightly browned. Cool slightly.

SPECIAL EXTRA

For a touch of sweetness, add 1 Tbsp. orange marmalade to cooked onion mixture before spooning over cream cheese mixture on pie crust.

LAYERED SUN-DRIED TOMATO AND ARTICHOKE SPREAD

PREP: 10 min. \ **TOTAL:** 1 hour 10 min. \ **MAKES:** 1½ cups or 12 servings, 2 Tbsp. each

1 **pkg. (8 oz.) *Philadelphia* Cream Cheese**

3 **Tbsp. finely chopped sun-dried tomatoes in oil, well drained**

3 **Tbsp. finely chopped drained canned artichoke hearts**

2 **Tbsp. pesto**

2 **Tbsp. chopped *Planters* Smoked Almonds**

2 **tsp. chopped fresh parsley**

1 **Cut** cream cheese horizontally into 3 slices using dental floss. (See Tip.) Place 1 slice on large sheet of plastic wrap; top with tomatoes and second cream cheese slice.

2 **Combine** artichokes and pesto; spoon over second cream cheese layer.

3 **Top** with remaining cream cheese slice, nuts and parsley; press nuts and parsley lightly into cream cheese to secure. Wrap with plastic wrap. Refrigerate 1 hour.

HOW TO CUT CREAM CHEESE WITH DENTAL FLOSS
Wrap 18-inch piece of dental floss around bottom third of cream cheese overlapping ends. Pull ends steadily to cut cream cheese. Repeat to make a total of 3 slices.

SERVING SUGGESTION
Serve with crackers.

SAVORY THREE-CHEESE SPREAD

PREP: 9 min. \ **TOTAL:** 10 min. \ **MAKES:** 10 servings

---

1 pkg. (8 oz.) *Philadelphia* Cream Cheese, softened

1 cup *Kraft* Shredded Cheddar Cheese

3 slices *Oscar Mayer* Smoked Ham, finely chopped

¼ cup *Kraft* Grated Parmesan Cheese

1 Tbsp. chopped red bell peppers

1 Tbsp. diagonally sliced green onions

¼ tsp. ground red pepper (cayenne)

1 **Spread** cream cheese onto bottom of 2½-cup microwaveable dish. Sprinkle with Cheddar cheese, ham and Parmesan cheese.

2 **Microwave** on HIGH 1 min. or until heated through.

3 **Top** with remaining ingredients.

SUBSTITUTE
Switch sliced jalapeño peppers, chopped roasted red peppers or *Taco Bell* Home Originals* Thick 'N Chunky Salsa for any of the toppings for a different flavor combo.

Taco Bell and *Home Originals* are trademarks owned and licensed by Taco Bell Corp.

SERVING SUGGESTION
Serve with crackers.

PARTY CHEESE BALL

PREP: 15 min. \ **TOTAL:** 3 hours 15 min. \ **MAKES:** 3 cups or 24 servings, 2 Tbsp. each

- 2 **pkg. (8 oz. each)** *Philadelphia* **Cream Cheese, softened**
- 1 **pkg. (8 oz.)** *Kraft* **Shredded Cheddar Cheese**
- 1 **Tbsp. finely chopped onions**
- 1 **Tbsp. chopped red peppers**
- 2 **tsp. Worcestershire sauce**
- 1 **tsp. lemon juice**
- ¼ **tsp. ground red pepper (cayenne)**
- 1 **cup chopped** *Planters* **Pecans, toasted**

1 **Beat** cream cheese and Cheddar in small bowl with mixer until well blended.

2 **Add** all remaining ingredients except nuts; mix well. Refrigerate several hours.

3 **Shape** into ball; roll in nuts.

SERVING SUGGESTION
Serve with crackers.

CUCUMBER ROULADES

PREP: 10 min. \ **TOTAL:** 10 min. \ **MAKES:** 6 servings

---

1 **English cucumber, peeled**

¼ **cup (¼ of 8-oz. tub)** *Philadelphia* **Chive & Onion Cream Cheese Spread**

1 **oz. smoked salmon, thinly sliced, cut into 12 pieces**

12 **sprigs fresh dill**

1 **Cut** cucumber into 12 thick slices. Use melon baller to scoop out center of each.

2 **Fill** with cream cheese spread; top with salmon and dill.

SUBSTITUTE
Substitute 12 drained canned baby shrimp for the salmon.

SAVORY PARMESAN BITES

PREP: 15 min. \ **TOTAL:** 30 min. \ **MAKES:** 32 servings

---

1 pkg. (8 oz.) *Philadelphia* Cream Cheese, softened

1 cup *Kraft* Grated Parmesan Cheese, divided

2 cans (8 oz. each) refrigerated crescent dinner rolls

1 cup chopped red peppers

¼ cup chopped fresh parsley

1 Heat oven to 350°F.

2 Beat cream cheese and ¾ cup Parmesan with mixer until well blended.

3 Separate dough into 8 rectangles; seal seams. Spread with cream cheese mixture; top with peppers and parsley. Fold each rectangle lengthwise into thirds to enclose filling; cut into 4 squares. Place, seam-sides down, on baking sheet; top with remaining Parmesan.

4 Bake 13 to 15 min. or until golden brown.